Cornerstones of Freedom

Mary McLeod Bethune

Patricia and Fred McKissack

CHILDRENS PRESS®

CHICAGO

Library of Congress Cataloging-in-Publication Data

McKissack, Pat, 1944-
  Mary McLeod Bethune / by Patricia and Fredrick
  McKissack.

    p.   cm.—(Cornerstones of freedom)
    Summary: Traces the life and achievements of the
black educator who fought bigotry and sought equality
for blacks in the areas of education and political rights.
    IBSN 0-516-06658-7
    1. Bethune, Mary McLeod, 1875-1955—Juvenile
literature. 2. Afro-Americans—Biography—Juvenile
literature. 3. Teachers—United States—Biography—
Juvenile literature. [1. Bethune, Mary McLeod,
1875-1955. 2. Teachers. Afro-Americans—Biography.]
I. McKissack, Fredrick. II Title. III. Series.
E185.97.B34M34 1992   92-12098
370'.092—dc20   CIP
[B]   AC

When Mary McLeod Bethune got off the train in Daytona, Florida, with her five-year-old son Bert, she had only $1.50 in her purse. Still, she was determined to start a school for young black girls. Lack of money was the least of her problems. It was 1904. She would have to overcome racism and discrimination, too. But Mary had been leaping over those obstacles all her young life.

Mary's parents, Samuel and Patsy McLeod, were former slaves. They had lived on the McIntosh plantation in Mayesville, South

Mary McLeod Bethune was greeted by a scene similar to this when she stepped off the train in Daytona in 1904.

A family picking cotton in the late 1800s

Carolina. After the Civil War ended, Samuel bought land from his old master and became a cotton farmer. Patsy worked as a cook to earn money for seeds and supplies.

Mary Jane McLeod was born on July 10, 1875. Although she was the McLeod's fifteenth child, she was special. She was their first free-born child. To Patsy and Samuel, freedom was an open door to unlimited possibilities.

The first few years of her life, Mary Jane was cared for by her grandmother, Sophia. All of the McLeod children were expected to work hard, and Mary Jane was no exception. As soon as she was old enough, she helped in the fields. Unlike her brothers and sisters, however, Mary Jane seemed to enjoy hard work.

Growing up surrounded by a large and loving family gave Mary Jane a healthy attitude and a lot of self-confidence. One day, however, something happened that left her hurt and confused. She went to work with her mother. The girl who lived there asked Mary to play. They enjoyed each other's company, until Mary Jane picked up a book. She turned a few pages, wondering what the words meant.

"Put that book down," the girl said. "Come over here and I'll show you some pictures. Put the book down. You can't read!"

Mary Jane was shocked. For the first time, her confidence was shaken. But not for long. That night, she remembered the harsh words. It was

The house in Mayesville where Mary McLeod Bethune was born

true. She couldn't read. Even so, she let her fingers trace the words in the family Bible. "God willing, I'll read one day," she whispered.

A while later, a visitor came to the McLeod farm. Mary Jane stopped working to watch the beautiful stranger walking toward them. The woman introduced herself as Miss Emma Wilson, the new schoolteacher. She explained that the Presbyterian Mission Board had sent her to Mayesville to start a school for black children. Miss Wilson asked if Mr. McLeod would allow his children to attend.

A school in Mayesville! Mary Jane was terribly excited. She almost blurted out, "Yes! Yes! I want to come to your school." However, that decision was up to her father.

Samuel pointed out that it was cotton-picking time. "I can't spare a set of hands," he said. Mary Jane looked at her mother with large, pleading eyes.

Patsy took Samuel aside. "We can spare one set of hands," she said, looking at Mary. "Let one of our children get a chance at learning."

Samuel nodded his agreement. "All right," he said, making it sound like it was his idea. "I think I'll let Mary Jane come to your school."

Mary Jane's brothers and sisters were disappointed when she couldn't read after the first day at school. But in time, Mary learned how to read. Her parents listened proudly as

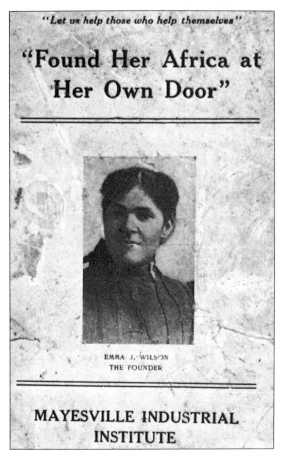

"Found Her Africa at Her Own Door"

EMMA J. WILSON
THE FOUNDER

MAYESVILLE INDUSTRIAL INSTITUTE

When missionary Emma Wilson (left) came to Mayesville in 1882 to start a school for black children, Samuel and Patsy McLeod (above) immediately allowed Mary to enroll.

their daughter read from the family Bible. She also recited poetry that Miss Wilson had taught the class. Mary was happy too, because now nobody could ever say, "You can't read!"

After the second year in Miss Wilson's school, Mary Jane could read and write very well. Sometimes she helped neighbors with their business papers. She was even able to help her father.

At the end of a harvest, farmers took their cotton to market, where it was weighed and sold. Every year, Samuel complained that his cotton weighed much less than he had expected it

An 1800s engraving showing cotton being weighed at the market

would. Unfortunately, he couldn't read the scales. So he had to accept what the clerk said.

One year, Mary went with her father to the cotton market. They stood in line together. The farmer in front of them lifted his cotton to the scales. The clerk said, "That's four hundred pounds." Mary saw that it was really five hundred pounds. That's why the farmers could never get ahead. They were being cheated! Mary Jane was furious.

Samuel was the next farmer in line. Mary Jane quickly thought of a way to help. Balancing the McLeod's cotton on the scales, the clerk reported, "You've got two hundred and eighty pounds on her, Sam." But Mary Jane, who had been watching the scales, exclaimed suddenly, "Isn't it four hundred and eighty pounds?" The clerk looked again.

"Right smart little girl you got there," the man said, gritting his teeth angrily. But, for the first time, Samuel got full price for his cotton—and even made a profit.

Miss Wilson's school went only to the sixth grade. Mary Jane was such a promising student that her teacher encouraged the McLeods to let their daughter continue her education at Scotia Seminary in Concord, North Carolina. This time, Samuel didn't need to be convinced. He and Patsy wanted their Mary Jane to go as far as she could in school.

Around that time, however, Samuel's mule died. He had to buy another one. There was no money left for school. Mary's dreams were shattered. She prayed for a miracle. Late one afternoon, Miss Wilson came running up the road, waving a letter. Excitement filled her voice as she read aloud from the letter. Mary Crissman, a seamstress from Denver, Colorado, had offered her life savings as a scholarship to one black child—and Mary had been the student selected. Miss Wilson had recommended her, feeling that her personal achievement and thirst for higher education made her the perfect candidate. The scholarship would take care of much of Mary's tuition. Years later, Mary wrote: "To this day my heart thrills with gratitude at the memory of that day. . . . A poor dressmaker, sewing for her daily bread, heard my call and came to my assistance. Out of her scanty earnings she invested in a life— my life!"

People in the community were proud that one of their own was going away to school. A group of friends and neighbors gathered at the Mayesville train station to say good-bye. They brought hair ribbons, handkerchiefs, scarves, and other parting gifts. As the train rolled away from the station, someone started a chorus of the song "Climbing Jacob's Ladder." It was quite a send-off for a twelve-year-old girl.

Mary arrived at Scotia Seminary in 1887. Boarding school was a strange and new experience for most of the students, and many became homesick and went home after one semester. Mary missed her family very much, and the work was hard, but she refused to give up. During the seven years that she lived and studied at Scotia, she learned math, science, English, social studies, Latin, home economics, and religion.

Days melted one into one another, until at last, Mary had accomplished her goals. Patsy and Samuel couldn't afford to attend Mary's graduation ceremony in 1894, but they were proud. Mrs. Crissman's graduation gift was a Bible that Mary kept all her life.

Mary McLeod and her Moody Bible Institute graduating class in 1895

Since the age of twelve, Mary had wanted to become a missionary in Africa. After graduating from Scotia Seminary, she immediately entered the Mission Training School of the Moody Bible Institute in Chicago. When she graduated from the institute in 1895, however, there were no openings for missionaries in Africa. Feeling very disappointed, Mary went back to Mayesville.

It was good to be home with her family again, but she was restless. She wanted to do something meaningful. After teaching for a while at Miss Wilson's school, Mary accepted a teaching position in Augusta, Georgia. After a productive year there, she transferred to a teaching job in

Sumter, South Carolina. While in Sumter, in 1898, Mary met and married Albertus Bethune. A year later, their son, Albert McLeod Bethune, was born.

Mary and Albertus moved to Palatka, Florida, in 1899. They helped build a mission school there. But Mary wanted to start her own school. She heard how terrible the living conditions were for black people in Daytona. There wasn't even a real school there. "That's where I'm needed," she thought. In 1904, against Albertus's wishes, Mary went to Daytona.

Now she had arrived. Things were as bad as she had been told. But she had no intention of turning back. "My whole life has been a series of miracles," Mrs. Bethune told Mrs. Susie Warren, the woman with whom she was staying while touring Daytona. Without hesitation, Mary announced that she had come to open a school

Daytona was becoming a resort town when Mary arrived in 1904.

for black girls. "Do you know of anybody who would rent me a place?" she asked.

With a loan from Mrs. Warren, Mary rented a small cottage on Oak Street for eleven dollars a month. The house was a mess, but Mary thought it was perfect. She and Bert would live in the two upstairs rooms, and the three downstairs rooms would become her school. It was a good start.

Daytona was rapidly becoming a resort town where wealthy northerners came to spend the winters. Besides enlisting the support of the black community, Mary also called upon some of these wealthy winter residents. If they agreed to listen, she proudly told them about her school. She was so enthusiastic that she was able to get people to invest in her dream.

On October 3, 1904, Mary McLeod Bethune opened Daytona Normal and Industrial Institute for Girls. She used boxes for desks. Her students wrote with charcoal on recycled paper found in the trash.

Five students, ranging in age from eight to twelve, showed up that first day. Mrs. Bethune greeted each girl with a big smile—just as Miss Wilson had welcomed her years earlier. She also offered a greeting that would become her trademark in the years to come: "Come in, little girl. We've been expecting you. I hope you will be happy with us." The school was open! Now she just had to keep it open.

A photo of Mary taken when she was in her twenties

Tuition was fifty cents a week, but that did not cover even half of the school's expenses. So, to raise money, Mrs. Bethune and her students made and sold ice cream and sweet-potato pies to railroad workers. They also formed a choir. The girls, dressed in blue skirts and white blouses, performed for guests who stayed at the large and fancy hotels and country clubs. Afterwards, Mrs. Bethune gave a brief presentation about her school, and then asked for donations.

School enrollment soared. Soon, there were more than one hundred children. Much more space was needed. To solve the problem, Mary bought a trash dump for $250. "That is where I will build my new school," she said.

Mrs. Bethune (first on right) visiting a school near Daytona in 1918

Mrs. Bethune used all her powers of persuasion to raise money for her school.

One evening, she stood looking at the dump. She didn't notice the old bedsprings, broken furniture, trash, and bottles littering the site. She saw her future school, and that made her smile. A passerby stopped and asked, "What do you see in all that junk?"

"Don't you see? it's my school," she answered.

The man looked at the debris. "I believe I do," he said.

Mrs. Bethune's dreams excited people of both races. Through her powers of persuasion, she quickly involved everyone she could in one or more of her projects. A number of very wealthy people, including oil magnate John D. Rockefeller and industrialist Henry J. Kaiser, made sizable donations to help Mrs. Bethune.

John D. Rockefeller

James Gamble

James Gamble, of Procter and Gamble, was so impressed after paying a visit to Mrs. Bethune that he immediately agreed to become chairman of the school's board of trustees. He became not only a lifelong benefactor, but also a devoted friend to Mary. The same was true of Thomas H. White, president of the White Sewing Machine Company. Many other people gave their support to the school as well. Those who couldn't give money donated their time and energy.

Construction of the new school proceeded slowly but steadily. In 1906, the school was moved from the house on Oak Street to its new quarters. The new building, still not quite finished, was named Faith Hall.

Soon Mary began hiring more teachers. "I can't pay you much," she told them honestly, "But I'll expect you to work like you're being paid a million dollars." Very few teachers turned her down.

Slowly, The School, as people began calling it, grew larger and stronger. A plot of land across the road from Faith Hall was purchased and turned into a working farm that brought in revenue for the school.

Unfortunately, Albertus didn't share Mary's dream. Although he came to Daytona, he soon grew tired of school work. He wanted to start his own business, so the couple chose to live apart.

In the early 1900s, the United States was a segregated country. One day in 1911, one of Mrs.

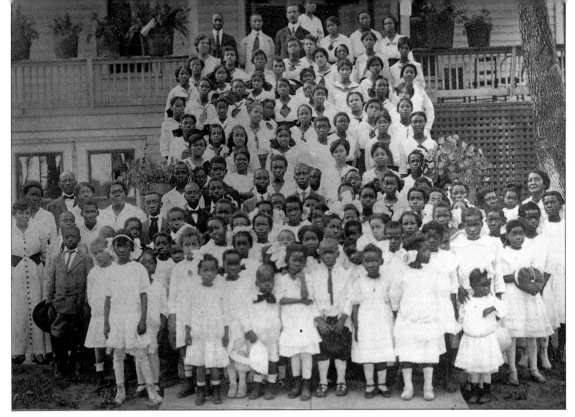

Mrs. Bethune and her staff and students on the steps of Faith Hall after Daytona Institute became coeducational

Bethune's students was refused treatment at an all-white hospital. In fact, in all of Florida, there was only one hospital that would admit black patients. Mrs. Bethune was outraged that blacks could not get decent medical treatment in Daytona. She decided that she must build a hospital for the city's black community.

In 1911, Dr. T. A. Adams, a graduate of Meharry Medical College in Nashville, Tennessee, helped Mrs. Bethune start a small, two-bed hospital. To honor her parents, Mary named it McLeod Hospital. After several years and many fund-raising projects, a larger facility was opened. McLeod Hospital provided health care for Daytona's blacks from 1913 to 1939. After that, the old building became Keyser Laboratory School, a teacher-training school. It was named in honor of Frances R. Keyser, a highly respected teacher from New York who had been one of Daytona Institute's first faculty members.

In 1914, Thomas White died. He had been an invaluable friend to Mrs. Bethune and one of the school's most faithful supporters. His death was deeply felt. It was Mr. White who had donated the money to complete Faith Hall in 1906. He had also used his influence to persuade the city of Daytona to extend water and electric services to the school. Wanting Mrs. Bethune to have a

An agriculture class at Keyser Labratory School in the 1930s

White Hall (above) was named in honor of Thomas H. White, one of Mrs. Bethune's most faithful friends and supporters.

place to call her own, he and Mr. Gamble had even bought her the small house behind Faith Hall that became known as the "Retreat." In his will, Mr. White had left the school $79,000. When a new administration building was completed in 1916, it was appropriately named White Hall.

Sometimes help came from unexpected sources. Every week, a wealthy widow named Flora B. Curtis bought a small amount of fresh vegetables from the school farm. Mrs. Curtis was always fussy and hard to please. The students who had to deal with her wondered if the few cents she spent each week were worth the aggravation, but Mrs. Bethune insisted that her students treat all customers with kindness and

Thomas H. White

respect. Each week, Mrs. Curtis was even sent a free copy of the *Advocate*, the school newspaper.

One day, Mrs. Curtis visited Mrs. Bethune. "I've been buying vegetables from you for some time now," she said.

"Yes, you have," answered Mrs. Bethune, taking out her account book. In a few minutes, she had totaled the entire amount Mrs. Curtis had spent over the years—about twenty dollars.

"Your students have always been so kind to me," Mrs. Curtis said. "I'm very particular, you know. I just wanted to say thank you."

Mrs. Bethune helped her visitor to the door. They never met again. Mrs. Curtis died shortly afterwards. It was soon discovered that she had willed $80,000 to the school! The money was used to build Curtis Hall, a new freshman dormitory that opened in 1922.

Flora B. Curtis Hall

Mary McLeod Bethune and members of the National Council of Negro Women

Mrs. Bethune spent a great deal of time managing school affairs. But she was also an active member of several educational and civil-rights organizations. She joined the National Association for the Advancement of Colored People and served as a board member of the Urban League. In addition, she served as president of the National Association of Colored Women, organized in 1896; and, in 1935, founded the National Council of Negro Women. Meanwhile, The School was doing well. But it could not continue to grow unless it received consistent financial support. Cookman Institute, an all-male black college in Jacksonville, Florida, had plenty of money, but it was dying.

Mrs. Bethune walks a picket line to protest racial discrimination.

Mrs. Bethune poses with a new graduate of Bethune-Cookman College

Enrollment was down, faculty turnover was high, and student morale was low. The officials at Cookman Institute knew that Mrs. Bethune's school had an excellent faculty and had experienced steady growth for nearly twenty years. They suggested to Mrs. Bethune that the two schools unite into one.

In 1923, Mrs. Bethune and the officials at Cookman began discussing a merger of the two schools. By 1925, the plans were completed. The newly formed, coeducational four-year college became known as Bethune-Cookman College. Mrs. Bethune became its first president. The Methodist Church took the responsibility for financial management and planning.

The merger allowed Mrs. Bethune to take a long overdue vacation. In 1927 she traveled to Europe. First she stopped in England. Then she went on to Scotland. She was thrilled to see places she had only read about. In Switzerland, she received a wonderful surprise. In her speeches, Mrs. Bethune had often said that the world was like a large flower garden. The different races of people were like flowers. One time, someone pointed out to her that there were no black flowers. After that, the analogy was spoiled for her. To her knowledge, no black flower existed.

While in Switzerland, she visited a garden in which roses of every color—including black roses—were all mixed up together on one hillside. The sight moved her deeply. For her, it symbolized the idea that black people, too, belonged in the world's "people-garden"; that all people, regardless of their color, should be allowed to flourish side by side.

Mrs. Bethune had often been called "the Black Rose." She took some black rose plants back to Florida, and had them planted at the entrance of her school. It reminded those who saw them that "just because you haven't seen a thing doesn't mean it doesn't exist."

In 1929, the bottom fell out of the American economy. When the stock market crashed, fortunes were lost. Poor people became even

Bethune-Cookman College, shown here today, was formed when Daytona Institute merged with Cookman Institute in 1923.

*In the 1930s and 1940s, Mrs. Bethune served as an advisor to
President Roosevelt on minority affairs.*

poorer. President Herbert Hoover invited Mrs.
Bethune to serve on the National Child Welfare
Commission. Her expertise in education and the
needs of minorities made her an invaluable
member of the commission.

In 1932, the American people elected Franklin
Delano Roosevelt president of the United States.
To rescue the economy, Roosevelt made sweeping
changes that became known as the New Deal.
His plan included government work projects
designed to put unemployed people back to
work. One of the New Deal programs was the
National Youth Administration, directed by
Aubrey Williams. The purpose of the NYA was to
give part-time employment to students who
wanted to continue their education.

President Roosevelt asked Mary McLeod Bethune to become director of the Office of Minority Affairs, a newly created branch of the NYA. At first, she declined. "I have to take care of my college," she protested. "I can't accept."

"I'm afraid you'll have to," President Roosevelt said simply, indicating how much he felt her help was needed.

Mrs. Bethune accepted the position. In so doing, she became the first black woman in the history of the United States to serve as a presidential advisor. She put as much energy into her new job as she had in building her school. She talked with the president frequently, giving him advice about minority issues. "I'm always glad to see you," President Roosevelt said.

"I wonder why," responded Mrs. Bethune. "I'm always asking for something."

The "Black Cabinet," made up of African-American political and civic leaders, was formed by Mrs. Bethune to address some of the problems of minority groups in the United States.

Mary McLeod Bethune and Eleanor Roosevelt became close friends.

"Yes," he replied, "but it's never for yourself."

A genuine friendship grew between First Lady Eleanor Roosevelt and Mrs. Bethune. It lasted as long as Mary lived. At the time, there were many bigoted people who thought that Mrs. Roosevelt should not entertain black people in the White House. The First Lady ignored her critics and continued to invite Mrs. Bethune and other African Americans to social gatherings.

Mrs. Bethune challenged the segregated system in other ways, too. In 1940, while a patient at Johns Hopkins Hospital, she insisted that a black doctor help with her surgery. There were no black doctors on staff. But one was found. Ever

During World War II, Mrs. Bethune helped select officer candidates for the Women's Army Corps.

since that day, Johns Hopkins has had an integrated staff.

When World War II began, the NYA was closed temporarily. At age seventy-five, Mrs. Bethune accepted a position as special assistant to the Secretary of War. She helped in the selection of black officer candidates in the Women's Army Corp (WAC).

President Roosevelt planned to hold a conference in San Francisco on April 25, 1945. The purpose was to write the charter for what would become the United Nations. The charter

As Mrs. Bethune and other black leaders look on, President Truman signs a document proclaiming February 1 as National Freedom Day.

would guarantee freedom and democracy to all the world's people. But Roosevelt died before the conference was held.

Mrs. Roosevelt and other members of the president's team continued as planned. Mrs. Bethune was invited to be part of the American delegation at the conference. Other blacks who attended were Walter White and W. E. B. Du Bois of the NAACP.

While in California, Mrs. Bethune spoke to thousands of schoolchildren. She told them about a world garden where there were flowers of all colors growing side by side. They were all

Mary McLeod Bethune,

Mrs. Bethune always encouraged young women to reach for the top.

Mrs. Bethune and her son, Albert

different, but each was just as beautiful as another. And yes, now there were black flowers growing in the garden. By then, the black tulip, orchid, and iris had been developed.

After the California trip, Mrs. Bethune retired from government service. However, she remained active in social and political organizations. She continued traveling, and spoke at conferences and conventions. Her son Bert and his family visited the Retreat often. When at home, she was surrounded by loving, caring students.

Mrs. Bethune died on May 18, 1955. Her gravestone is marked simply "MOTHER." In 1904,

30

the world had taken little notice of a young teacher named Mary Bethune. But when she died, Mrs. Bethune was mourned by the world.

In her will, Mary MacLeod Bethune wrote: "My worldly possessions are few. Yet, my experiences have been rich. From them I distilled principles and policies in which I firmly believe. . . . Here, then is my legacy: I LEAVE YOU LOVE . . . HOPE . . . A THIRST FOR EDUCATION . . . FAITH . . . RACIAL DIGNITY . . . A DESIRE TO LIVE HARMONIOUSLY WITH YOUR FELLOW MEN . . . and, finally, A RESPONSIBILITY TO OUR YOUNG PEOPLE."

A postage stamp issued in Mrs. Bethune's honor

Mary McLeod Bethune

INDEX

Adams, Dr. T. A., 17
Bethune, Albert McLeod, 12, 30
Bethune, Albertus, 12, 13, 16
Bethune-Cookman College, 22
choir, 14
Cookman Institute, 21-22
Crissman, Mary, 9
Curtis, Flora B., 19, 20
Curtis Hall, 20
Daytona, Florida, 3, 12, 13, 16, 17, 18
Daytona Normal and Industrial Institute for Girls, 13, 14, 15, 16, 18, 19, 20, 21
Du Bois, W. E. B., 28
Faith Hall, 16, 18, 19
Gamble, James, 16, 19
Hoover, Herbert, 24
Jacksonville, Florida, 21
Johns Hopkins Hospital, 26, 27
Kaiser, Henry J., 15
Keyser, Frances R., 18
Keyser Laboratory School, 18

McLeod, Samuel, 3, 4, 6, 7, 8, 9, 10
McLeod, Patsy, 3, 4, 6, 9, 10
McLeod Hospital, 17, 18
Mayesville, South Carolina, 3-4, 6, 10, 11
Meharry Medical College, 17
Methodist Church, 22
Moody Bible Institute, 11
National Association for the Advancement of Colored People (NAACP), 21, 28
National Association of Colored Women, 21
National Child Welfare Commission, 24
National Council of Negro Women, 21
National Youth Administration, 24, 25, 27
New Deal, 24
Office of Minority Affairs, 25
Palatka, Florida, 12

"people garden," 22-23, 28, 30
Presbyterian Mission Board, 6
"Retreat," 19, 30
Rockefeller, John D., 15
Roosevelt, Eleanor, 26, 28
Roosevelt, Franklin Delano, 24, 25, 27
school, 3, 6, 7, 9, 10, 11, 12
Scotia Seminary, 9, 10, 11
stock market crash, 23-24
Sumter, South Carolina, 12
Switzerland, 22
United Nations, 27-28
Urban League, 21
Warren, Susie, 12, 13
White, Thomas H, 16, 18, 19
White, Walter, 28
White Hall, 19
Williams, Aubrey, 24
Wilson, Emma, 6, 7, 9, 11, 13
Women's Army Corps (WAC), 27
World War II, 27

PHOTO CREDITS

Cover, National Portrait Gallery, Washington, D.C./Art Resource, NY; 1, Culver Pictures; 2, Library of Congress; 3, The Bettmann Archive; 4, Picture Bank; 5, Bethune-Cookman College; 7 (left), Culver Pictures; 7 (right), Bethune-Cookman College; 8, Courtesy of the South Carolina Historical Society; 11, Moody Bible Institute; 12, The Bettmann Archive; 13, 14, Bethune-Cookman College; 15 (top), Moorland-Spingarn Research Center, Howard University; 15 (bottom), North Wind; 16, Courtesy of the Cincinnati Historical Society; 17, 18, 19 (top), Bethune-Cookman College; 19 (bottom), The Western Reserve Historical Society, Cleveland, Ohio; 20, Schomburg Center for Research in Black Culture, The New York Public Library, Astor, Lenox and Tilden Foundations; 21 (top), Bethune-Cookman College; 21 (bottom), Moorland-Spingarn Research Center, Howard University; 22, 23, Bethune-Cookman College; 24, Wide World; 25, Bethune Museum and Archives, Washington, D.C., photographed by Scurlock Photographers; 26, Bethune-Cookman College; 27, Schomburg Center for Research in Black Culture, The New York Public Library, Astor, Lenox, and Tilden Foundations; 28, UPI/Bettmann; 29, Bethune-Cookman College; 30 (top), Schomburg Center for Research in Black Culture, New York Public Library, Astor, Lenox and Tilden Foundations; 30 (bottom), 31 (bottom), Bethune-Cookman College

Picture Identifications:
Cover: A portrait of Mary McLeod Bethune by Betsy G. Reyneau
Page 1: Mrs. Bethune speaking at the American-Soviet Friendship rally in 1944
Page 2: Mrs. Bethune stands in front of her home–known as
The Retreat–on her last day as president of Bethune-Cookman College in
1943; she was resigning to devote more time to government service
Page 29: Mrs. Bethune outside the Capitol in Washington, D.C.

Project Editor: Shari Joffe
Designer: Karen Yops
Cornerstones of Freedom Logo: David Cunningham

ABOUT THE AUTHORS

Patricia and Fred McKissack are award-winning authors whose titles have been honored with the Coretta Scott King Award, the Jane Addams Peace Award, and the Parent's Choice Award. Pat's book *Mirandy and Brother Wind*, illustrated by Jerry Pinkney, was a 1989 Caldecott Honor Book. The McKissacks have authored more than twenty books for Childrens Press.